JavaScript

Basic Fundamental Guide for Beginners

TABLE OF CONTENTS

Introduction

Congratulations on purchasing *JavaScript : Basic Fundamental Guide for Beginners* and thank you for doing so.

The following chapters will discuss how to program using JavaScript. We're going to start from the very beginning and explain program logic as we make our way through this broad topic and try to uncover everything as possible.

JavaScript is immensely popular. Therefore, you're doing the right thing by trying to learn it. My goal is to give you all of the tools and information you need to become a fantastic JavaScript programmer in no time at all.

There are plenty of books on this subject on the market. Thanks again for choosing this one! Every effort was made to ensure that this book is packed with useful information. Please enjoy!

Chapter 1

History of JavaScript

This book is going to tackle a couple of hefty questions and also assume that you've got little to no practical programming experience. The reason for this is that, for a lot of people, JavaScript is their first language. Many people start out with something like web development or perhaps with a recommendation from a friend and find that JavaScript is one of the "easiest" languages to learn.

This is a bit of a misnomer of course; I've helped a lot of people learn to program. Some benefit more from a language that is more abstract and easier to understand, such as JavaScript. Others still benefit more from languages where everything is a concept and put right in front of them to toy with, because the verbosity helps them to understand what they're working within a better sense, such as Java or C++.

Regardless of these, I'm going to assume, since you're here, that you're in the first camp, as well as explain things with enough rigor so that you'll still understand the language well if you're already in the second camp. JavaScript is not a difficult first language. Actually, it's far from it. It's easy to understand, abstract, and master. However, there is a definite degree of challenge that comes with, such as getting out of your comfort zone and learning all of the little concepts related to programming itself.

Therefore, let's think for a second. What is JavaScript? JavaScript is a programming language. A programming language is basically something that allows you to talk to computers and instruct them on what to do. We know for a fact that computers don't understand English. In fact, they don't even understand programming languages.

When you break it down, you'll find that computers only really understand things in terms of binary codes - a sequence of ones and zeroes. This is where the name of the computer comes from a *computer*.

The computer makes millions of tiny computations that you can't see every single second. All of these computations are performed using these ones and zeroes that are present at the very smallest level of the computer that you can't see. Knowing this, we've figured out over the years that these ones and zeroes could be controlled and manipulated, first, through the development of languages that work with the processor of the computer itself (assembly) and, second, through the development of languages that serve as the connection between the complex zeroes and ones and the programmer.

As computers have gotten more popular and stronger these days, people who are interested in programming want to learn languages that aren't absurdly difficult to use and understand. As a result, over time, programming languages too have become much simpler as more people started programming as a hobby. The increased processing power of computers over the years and the standardization of an object-oriented paradigm have led to the development of far simpler languages.

In order to understand JavaScript itself, we have to first learn it's history. In the 1970s, there was a place called Bell Labs, a research lab owned and managed by AT&T. A lot of important technological advances originated from Bell Labs. One of the most important ones that you've probably heard before is the *Unix* system.

Unix was a landmark. It was an open-source and simple operating system that was intuitive enough that it could easily be marketed to businesses, developers, and universities all in tandem with one another without encroaching on each other's markets. This was spurred by the development of the C programming language.

3

The C programming language itself has it's long line of history, but essentially it was the first simple and intuitive language that almost anybody can figure out. It offers a layer of abstraction from the system itself and also offers the programmer the ability to scrutinize the system buildup and therefore understand the computer much better. This allows the programmer to directly manage things, such as memory allocation, or the amount of memory being used by the program in order to perform certain processes. In short, C allows programmers to better understand the system. However, they are expected to handle a great amount of difficult information and are prone to manipulate, for example, the computer's processing capabilities.

Unix would eventually be rewritten in C instead of the standard Assembly code. This is part of the reason why C became so famous. This was a huge deal because it means that any processor that can run a C compiler, that is, the program which converts human-readable programming code to Assembly code that the computer can understand can run Unix as well. Now, this program can be compiled in any system that has a C compiler. This made the program extremely popular worldwide.

Moreover, since C is open source, universities often teach their students the language so that even if they cannot immediately compile Unix for their computers, they can at least modify the code so that they *can* run Unix on them. In addition, Unix is beneficial to C and vice versa because, first, C is being taught in universities to allow students to gain experience first before handling their Unix courses and, second, because Unix comes with a C compiler which makes it even easier for people to write and run codes on Unix systems.

This may seem like an irrelevant detail, but it's a pretty important factor in the overall development of JavaScript and is a key part in the development of modern programming languages in general. This is because these languages can inspire a ton of different languages. For example, the extremely popular languages Java, Python, and C++ all have been – to one extent or another – inspired by C.

JavaScript is no exception. However, with that context, let's think back what the computing landscape was like in the late 80s and early 90s. The general population was slowly being introduced with computers because of the popularity of both C and Unix. The combined popularity and accessibility of these mean that a lot of applications are being built for a lot of computers, approximately exponentially more every year.

However, the Internet was still in its infancy in many ways. Web browsers, for example, were unpopular and nowhere near their technological peak. Web browsers were, in many ways, much more simple and unsophisticated as were web pages themselves.

Currently, web pages primarily consist of just basic text markup rendered through HTML. This book isn't going to tackle HTML except when it's necessary. Therefore, a working knowledge about it is assumed. JavaScript is, after all, one of the three core web development languages alongside HTML and CSS. So, it's worthwhile to learn HTML and CSS as well.

Anyhow, early web browsers were known as *static web pages*. Static web pages are the opposite of *dynamic* web pages, which are web pages that are designed to reflect and render text and images only. Basically, once a static web page is loaded, it cannot be changed from within the page without changing and the reloading the *web file*.

Dynamic web pages – or pages that can be changed in real-time without altering the web file itself – are implemented through what is called *client-side scripting*. Client-side scripting is about allowing changes to happen on a web page exclusively on the browser side. That is, client-side scripting allows sophisticated logic and dynamic changes to run within the context of the user's web browser. Any changes are made their machine and within their browser and don't necessarily indicate the transfer of information to a server.

Essentially, JavaScript and all related languages are about giving life to web pages. It's about taking web pages and making them able to do things instead of just be still. This functionality was, for a long time, just a glimmer in the eye of people who were looking forward to web development. However, this doesn't mean that scripting didn't exist way before. There was early support for technologies designed to allow web pages to interact more. However, these were very rudimentary. The early graphical web browsers were capable of scripting even during its infancy.

This resulted in the creation of another browser, *Mozilla* which inspired the development of Firefox. Currently, however, Firefox was far from being a factor. Officially, the browser was released as *Netscape*, which was known by many as being among the most popular browsers in the 90s, and if you used a computer in the 90s, then you probably were using Netscape.

In the mid-90s, the idea of embedded codes in web pages – that is, codes written in other programming languages that can be inserted directly into and run from a web page – started becoming even more popular. However, there still wasn't enough information regarding the process of practical embedded languages. Java did somewhat serve the purpose, but it wasn't simple. In fact, it died out because it entails a great amount of raw computing power for it to be used. A better alternative was needed, something that can be directly embedded into and alter the web page. Such a thing didn't exist.

Netscape decided to create a scripting language that can run within HTML documents and be easily embedded and interpreted within the browser itself. The language was supposed to display a similar syntax to Java and C++. This was to differentiate it from other popular scripting languages at that time, such as Perl, Python, and Lisp.

6

Believe it or not, a C-inspired scripting language was relatively nouveau at the time.

The language was first released as LiveScript and then later was changed to *JavaScript*. JavaScript became the final name of the language from that on, most likely as an attempt by Netscape to capitalize the success of the Java programming language that was extremely popular at the time, even though JavaScript wasn't particularly related to Java except in its syntactic in some places.

JavaScript was initially only implemented for client-side scripting or the creation of dynamic web pages (as we've already discussed). The first server-side implementation of JavaScript appeared a year or so after the initial release of JavaScript. Today, the server-side JavaScript is still being implemented even though its implementations are far less common than those of the client-side.

The mid-90s showed the development of many now-important web technologies and also browser wars. JavaScript plays an important part in the browser wars, which gained popularity pretty quickly and was implemented by Netscape in their browser. However, Netscape's primary opponent during that time, Internet Explorer, didn't have a support for JavaScript.

This started to change in late 1996. It was clear that some kind of business-wide standard for JavaScript was needed in order for the World Wide Web to be accessed by all browsers. In order to do this, Netscape sent their language into a standards board in order for the language to be reviewed and standardized. The language standard was called ECMAScript, which was published in 1997. This standardization became the starting point for many different languages and is a language in its own right. It's the *standard* of a language, upon which other languages are derived from. All of these different derivations are referred to as *implementations* of the standard. JavaScript is the most popular one, but there were a few others that transpired, such as ActionScript designed for Flash coding.

With the standardization of ECMAScript, JavaScript was finally being used by other browsers and not just Netscape. JavaScript was an ambition in the mid-2000s. During this time, JavaScript and the things for which it could be used were becoming popular to the public (especially the developers) after the development of a white paper wherein Ajax was defined, basically promising the development of extremely dynamic web pages as opposed to the static pages prior. This resulted in the development of many more technologies that can be used alongside JavaScript, such as jQuery, which remained until 2015 or 2016.

A little later in the Oughts, there was at last cohesive work done in order to push the status of the JavaScript language forward and force new standards fit for new technologies. Since then, newer implementations and constant unified updates have been created to develop a unified version of ECMAScript. Therefore, all implementations of ECMA, including JavaScript, resulted in the development of more technical possibilities.

For the last few years, new standards of ECMAScript have been released every year.

The major breakthrough of JavaScript must have been Ajax when developers began to take interest and supported the language. Today, there is an even greater need for an extensive browser support, and JavaScript began to push for that spotlight. Since then, it has become the most widely used web scripting language.

The history of JavaScript shows that it has undergone challenges to become what it is today. I hope that you appreciated the path that it has taken. In the following chapter, we're going to discuss exactly where we *are* at today and all of the different things that JavaScript can be used for.

Chapter 2

How JavaScript is Used

Currently, JavaScript is used for a number of different uses in the mainstream web framework. It is implemented through a number of different layers like *React.js* or *Bootstrap.js*.

Raw JavaScript is fairly uncommon today and is used only to build bigger projects and APIs. Many of these are open source, and you will encounter raw JavaScript generally whenever you're working with these open source projects and not so often in your raw code.

For a long time – though not so often now – jQuery was one of the most popular JavaScript libraries, if not the most popular. You can still sometimes find it lingering around, but it has largely been outpaced by other more popular web frameworks.

This introduces the most popular use of JavaScript, its implementation among other Ajax interfaces and various different web-based frameworks which allow you to create stunning and dynamic web pages. Raw JavaScript, as I said, isn't terribly popular, but you're going to encounter a lot of challenges when using this.

JavaScript is also commonly used with HTML5 and CSS3 to create browser-based games. These are becoming more popular as web pages are becoming increasingly capable of running complex animations. JavaScript offers a fantastic catalyst to all of these because it allows the formation of client-side scripts.

Don't misunderstand; knowing how JavaScript works is extremely useful. You can use this knowledge as a catalyst to other things. Once you're finished with this book, I'd recommend that you start looking into the various web frameworks that use JavaScript. There are numerous.

React.JS, Meteor.JS, Mithril.JS, and Vue.JS are all extremely popular because they allow you to easily build interactive and dynamic web pages. In the modern day, this is an extremely important utility and will greatly benefit you as a programmer.

You'll also find that Node.JS offers a solid server-side scripting implementation. It can stand against PHP as one of the more popular web-based server-side technologies, even though it's much younger than PHP. If you're interested in running your servers and queries efficiently and building generally broad web-based applications, then Node.JS is preferred.

Now, we're going to discuss how to program in raw JavaScript, which will prepare you for using any of these. Having a foundation in programming is incredibly important.

Chapter 3

How to Program in JavaScript

In this chapter, we're going to start diving into how one can program in JavaScript. There is a lot to cover in this chapter. So, we're going to start from the basics and work our way up as we cover all of the different topics and try to build a finite idea of what this language is capable of. By the end of this chapter, you're going to understand a plethora of different concepts related to programming. Strap in tight because this is where the bulk of the book is going to come in.

Setting Up

Setting up JavaScript is incredibly easy. If you have a web browser, then you have JavaScript. It's as simple as that. Web browsers have built-in implementation engines for JavaScript, as does any other programs that purport to run JavaScript, such as the game engines that we mentioned.

This means that running JavaScript doesn't entail you to do much. However, there is one thing that we need to take note of before we continue. While normally you can save JavaScript files on their own and work on them in that way, you can't debug them in a browser like this. In order to use your JavaScript in your browser and have your scripts run, you need to call those scripts in one way or another. In order to simplify this, we're going to create an HTML document using the script tags. Write the following code in a new file called first.htm:

11

```
<html>
<head>
  <script>
        document.write("Hello world!\n");
  </script>
</head>
<body>
</body>
</html>
```

Go ahead and save this file and then open it in the web browser of your choice. You'll see the following:

Hello world!

With this, bravo! You've written your first JavaScript script. So, you may be wondering, what is the essential difference between putting data within your file's head tags and your file's body tags?

The head tag is usually reserved for any programmatic logic in HTML. You can put the script in your body tag, and it will work equally well. However, most of the time, the JavaScript would be saved to a *different* file and then from there be loaded into the web page rather than all of it being confined in the same HTML document. This is the simplest way of emulating this sort of functionality within the confines that we've currently developed.

Data and Variables

At this point, we will talk about a concept that's a little bit heftier: the concept of *data*, *value*, and *variables*. You're going to see these all the time in programming. So, it's important that we start to talk about it a little bit. Depending on how and why you're going to use JavaScript, this may not come up so much. It will still come up, for example, if you're going to focus primarily on modern web development but often in a more abstracted way. However, nonetheless, it's important that we cover this concept because it's foundational to pretty much in all programming, in addition to the fact that this concept is instrumental in understanding some of the later concepts that we're going to be covering. For this reason, we're going to go ahead and just assume that we need to learn it and do that.

So, let's start with a simpler quest before anything else: what is a value? In order to understand the other concepts here, you need to understand how computers process data. As we said in the very first chapter, computers don't understand things like humans do. Ultimately, they process things in a series of mathematical equations, after things have been abstracted into things that resemble nothing like the value which we gave. For example, the bitwise representation of any given number won't really resemble the number that was passed in. Likewise, when you're trying to work with characters and text on-screen, computers have no innate bearing on what any of this is or how it can be used; they don't have the innate capacity for language that we do. All they understand is calculations. So, they need a method by which they can take these abstract human concepts and convert them into smaller numbers that *they* can work with.

However, that doesn't really answer or question. It only gives an entry point. The point that I'm trying to make is that in the end, computers understand all different representations of ideas in different ways, whether those ideas are numbers, letters, or any other thing that you can form some kind of abstract idea out of.

All of these abstract ideas form the nucleus of an idea that is a little bigger – the idea of the *value*. A value is any given abstract representation of some idea. That value could be a number, a character, a set of characters, or none of the above. A value is the communication of an abstract idea that can *be* communicated.

Computers understand these values according to the *type* of value they are. Computers need different types because, again, all of the values that a computer can understand need to be converted from our abstract idea of these values into something that the computer can work with, that is, ones and zeroes. These separate kinds of data can be referred to succinctly as *data types*.

There are numerous different data types in JavaScript, and there even exists the ability to create your own. However, data types are a little bit like atoms; there comes a point where if you break a molecule down that is composed of different atoms, then eventually you just get singular atoms and can't go any further without getting to the subatomic level and dealing with things like particles and quarks and so forth.

Data types in JavaScript and programming, in general, are a bit the same. Every programming language has these nucleic data types that form the basis for all other kinds of data in the programming language. These types that can't be broken down any further are called *primitive* types, and every language has their own primitive types.

JavaScript specifically has six different primitive types, each with their own use cases and definitions. Here, we're going to talk about what these different primitive types are so that you will know what these primitive types can *do* and what different kinds of data you can store and manipulate in JavaScript.

string – String denotes a data type which is necessarily composed of just characters. Character here refers to anything that is alphanumeric or symbolic. Basically, character is any text which may be represented on a screen in a computer. String refers explicitly to the idea of these characters and not necessarily to the characters themselves. For example, if you have a string value that hold numbers, then you cannot add a given number to it, because the string numeric value will not be understood by the system as numbers themselves but just as a set of characters which represent numbers. This idea will make a bit more sense later on when we start discussing the idea of arrays.

number – Number denotes a data type that uses *any* number, whether those are whole, decimal, or any other kind of number. This slightly separates JavaScript from other programming languages. We'll talk about this more in-depth a little bit later on, but it's a pretty easy concept to grasp, so don't stress about it too much.

undefined – Undefined is the data type which belongs to any variable (which we'll discuss in a second) that doesn't have a value set to it just yet. *undefined* can also be returned in a given function, but we'll talk about that later as well when we start talking about functions in general.

null – Null in computer science refers to any number which doesn't *have* a value. Null is different from undefined because undefined values simply generally haven't had a value ascribed to them yet, whereas null finitely doesn't have a value affixed.

boolean – Booleans are another concept that will make more sense later on but for right now just understand booleans as pertaining to the idea of true or false. Booleans are thereby a little bit of a rougher concept to really completely understand, even if they appear incredibly simple.

symbol – Symbols are the hardest primitive to understand for a beginner, and, frankly, as a beginner, you aren't really going to need to know about them. So you can just forget about them for the time being. However, for necessity's sake, we needed to cover it.

All of these also have *object* wrappers, which are another concept we'll talk about later in the chapter. I know, I know, it seems like I'm introducing a whole lot of ideas without talking about them at all, but don't worry. I promise we'll get to *all* of this in due time.

So why is this information important? What can one do with this knowledge? Well, you can do a whole lot. For example, let's change the code that we had so that the document.write line reads like the following:

```
document.write(4 + 3);
```

Save your file and refresh the page. You should be seeing the following:

```
7
```

See how intuitive that is? You can manipulate these pieces of data. We'll get to that in just a second after we talk about *variables*. Now that you know how data works, you're somewhat prepared to start working with this next concept. See, sometimes, obviously, you're going to want to keep data for more than just one instance as we did above. In these cases, you need a way to keep track of data.

This functionality is offered to you through *variables*. You can keep track of data using variables and then change the data later by referring to it by some name that you define. You can define variables in JavaScript as the following:

```
var variableName;
```

You can also define it with an initial value. This is called initialization:

```
var myBananas = 3;
```

Alternatively, you can declare a variable and then define its value later:

```
var myBananas;
myBananas = 3;
```

So, why does all of this go together? First, the reason why we need to talk about data types was that JavaScript doesn't make you keep up with what kind of data a variable holds. This is good in some ways because it honestly makes it a much easier language to learn that it might be otherwise compared to something like C++ where you have to explicitly declare what type of data you're working with. Meanwhile, this can be difficult for a beginner who doesn't exactly understand how data works and how computers understand data. So, let's just assume that you're still starting to learn JavaScript. I decided that it's best to discuss how all of this works as opposed to just throwing you into the fire and expecting you to figure it out on your own. I may have just saved you a bit of time and future troubleshooting!

You can print out variables the same way you can print out individual data. This is because variables essentially just serve as boxes which can hold values. You can reach into these boxes and change the values, but the box will retain the same number of variable and refer to whatever is placed within it. When you create a variable, you're creating a box which may hold values. When you refer to that variable, you're saying "hey, whatever is in the box with that name, I want to work with that."

Let's try this with the last piece of data. Change your script as follows:

```
var number1 = 4;
var number2 = 4;
var number3 = number1 + number2;
document.write(number3);
```

Save it and reload the page; you'll end up with the following:

```
8
```

If that's the case, then perfect! You're well on your way to being adept at JavaScript. This is only the beginning, but much more can be done from here.

You can create a string variable by assigning a value with quotes around it; quotes indicate that a value is a string value. Note, too, that when you create these variables in JavaScript, they aren't created as the primitives but rather as the object wrappers – which, again, we'll talk about more in-depth later. When you try to connect strings, you do what's called a *concatenation*, which is where the characters from both of the strings are put together into one bigger string.

Anyhow, it's time that we move on to the next major part of this chapter, which uses all the knowledge we gained so far. We need to start discussing *math*.

Math in JavaScript

Math in JavaScript isn't a terrible complicated thing. For the most part, it uses symbols that you're likely already familiar with. There won't be a whole lot for you to learn here, but rather this section is about taking the parts that you're most likely probably already familiar with and then using those in order to build a better base.

Math operations in JavaScript are written and carried out through the use of mathematical operators. These often will be very similar to their counterparts in other languages and, indeed, in math in general.

The operators in JavaScript are as follows:

    a + b

This is the *addition* operator, as you've already seen. This will add two things together. It can also be used to concatenate strings or to connect them. If you add a number to a string, then the number will be added *to* the string; for example "hello " + 5 would equal "hello 5."

    a - b

This is the *subtraction* operator. The subtraction operator is used to subtract one value from another, as you might predict.

    a * b

This is the *multiplication* operator. This is used to multiply one thing by another.

    a / b

This is the *division* operator. This is used to divide one number by another.

    a % b

This is the modulo operator. This is used to find the remainder of a certain equation. For example, 5 % 2 would return 1 since 5 / 2 would give a remainder of 1.

    a**b

This is the exponentiation operator. The exponentiation operator will raise a "to the power" of b and return that number.

These are the basic mathematical operators of JavaScript. You can use these to easily perform complex mathematical operations in JavaScript. This may not seem like a big deal right now, but as we press on through the chapter, you'll see why math, more or less, is essential in anything you may do with JavaScript (or programming in general).

The other important operators to cover are the assignment operators. You can use the assignment operators in order to change a value in shorthand.

Assignment operators take a variable and then use any of the above operators with an equals sign. This will assign a new value to that variable. The most obvious assignment operator is the *equals sign*, which is used to assign a value to the left variable of the right side of the expression.

a += b

This is equal to a = a + b.

a -= b

This is equal to a = a - b.

a *= b

This is equal to a = a * b.

a /= b

This is equal to a = a / b.

a %= b

This is equal to a = a % b.

There are two more shorthand operators, the increment and decrement operators. These can be used to add or subtract one from a given variable, *a++* and *a--*, respectively, where *a* is the name of the variable that you're trying to increment or decrement.

We've covered most of the basic arithmetic and assignment operators that you're going to need for JavaScript. Now we're going to use this knowledge to build a foundation for understanding programmatic logic, which is a great and important foundation for being able to use all these.

Foundations of Logic

So, why do we need to focus on logic specifically? What do we have to gain from it? The simple answer is that understanding logic allows you to let your computer understand logic. All of logic may be expressed in a mathematical way, and your computer, too, may come to understand logic in that sense. Computers, after all, are excellent at solving equations and able to make comparisons as a result of those equations.

This may not seem like a huge deal, but computers being able to think is a really good thing. Think about it; any time that your program is able to decide technically, it's using logic. You may not even have to think that hard. There are a lot of basic instances of logic. This will make more sense later on.

So what exactly is logic? Logic is, in one way or another, just a manner of systematically using statements. These statements can then be used to derive conclusions. Logic is used, often, in order to determine whether a given statement is true or false, both in computing and in real life.

Perhaps the most classic example of logic is in the old Socratic form: "All men are mortal; Socrates is a man; therefore, Socrates is mortal." This sort of transitive logic provides the foundation for much of what we know about *modern* logic and is perhaps one of the best examples of simple applications of logic used in different contexts.

Logic in computers is usually based on *expressions*. Expressions might be familiar to you from your old high school or college algebra courses, where you write out a certain statement written and determine if it's true or false. You can use algebra on these expressions to simplify them just by treating the expression operator as an equals sign.

This basic format stays the same. Expressions are essentially a method by which you can compare one value to another. You can set the standard of the comparison, for example, whether you're determining if two values are equivalent or not, if one is more or less than the other, so on. Expressions, therefore, are a great tool used in logic and play a part likewise in computer-based logic.

You form expressions through the use of logical operators. These logical operators are the very basis of expressions. The following are the logical operators that you can use in JavaScript:

$a == b$

This will compare value *a* to value *b* and return whether or not the two are equal to each other. If so, it will return true and false if otherwise.

$a === b$

This will compare the two values and return true if they are both equal to each other *and* if they are of the same type.

$a != b$

This will compare the two values and return true if they are *not* equal to each other *or* if they are not of the same type. This is logical *or*. So, they can be both *unequal* and *of the same type,* and it will still return true. I'll explain that later.

$a > b$

This will determine if a is greater than b.

$a < b$

This will determine if a is less than b.

$a >= b$

This will determine if a is greater than or equal to b.

a <= b

This will determine if a is less than or equal to b.

You can use these to form *individual expressions*. You can then use these expressions in logical statements, which will be discussed later. Note how these expressions return either true or false depending on whether they're true or not. This goes back to the boolean values that we discussed earlier. These return a boolean value, which may be either true or false depending on the statement.

Let's return to variables for a second. You can store a boolean value to a variable, like the following:

val myBool = true;

However, you can also store an *expression* to a variable, and it will store the true or false boolean value.

val myBool = 3 > 5;

The above would be false because 3 is obviously *not* greater than 5. Remember that the function of expressions is to compare values; therefore, you can compare any values. You can likewise compare variables instead of raw values. Make sure your variables are of the same type. If not, you might see some weird results in your comparison!

Anyway, you can chain these expressions into a longer expression to build more sophisticated logical systems. These systems will check *every* part of the greater expression to verify whether or not the logic behind them is true or not.

There are three more logical operators that we haven't covered yet which are tailored specifically toward the purpose of allowing you to build these larger expressions.

expressionA && expressionB

This is the logical *and* operator which checks if both expressions A and B are true. If so, the entire expression will return true and false if otherwise.

expressionA || expressionB

This is the logical *or* operator which checks if *either* expression A *or* B is true. If neither is true, then the entire expression will return false. If either expression is true, then the entire expression will return true. If, technically, one expression is true and the whole expression is true, then both expressions may be true since the technical limitation shows that either side is true and that it is satisfied even if both sides are true.

!(expression)

This is the logical, *not* operator. You can use this to test whether something is *not* true. If it's *not* true, then the entire expression will return true. If it *is* true, then the entire expression will return false.

Note that when you use these, you have to use the exact version that I've specified. For example, getting two equals signs but using one instead will significantly change the meaning of your expression. Likewise, using only one ampersand (&) or one pipe (|) sign will change the meaning of your expression at its very root by transforming it into a bitwise expression, that is, it will be evaluating things at the bit level or the smallest possible mathematical level that you're allowed access to by your computer. You cannot obtain the results that you wanted, *unless* you're specifically trying to do bitwise operations which, at this point, you almost certainly cannot. Just be cautious when working with these expressions.

With that said, hopefully, we've built a solid foundation of logical understanding. This is important because it's going to play a great role in the following sections of the chapter where we discuss the actual meat of control flow and all of the topics that make it up.

Control Flow 101: Conditional Statements

That foray into control flow starts right as we speak. We're going to discuss how you can use the expressions that we covered in the last part of this chapter to build conditional statements. Conditional statements are the first essential part of control flow.

You may be wondering what control flow is. Control flow is the method by which you can direct your computer to obtain rudimentary forms of logic. By using the control flow, you can direct your computer (for instance, your web page) to make different decisions based on the current state of the given data.

Conditional statements exist in two forms, active and passive conditionals. Passive conditionals are the most basic form. So, we're going to be covering those first.

Passive conditionals are based on the idea of evaluating a single expression and then taking action if it's true. If it's true, then the code within will be run. If the condition is evaluated and turns out to not be true, then the code will be skipped over.

The basic form of a passive conditional in control flow is as follows:

```
if (expression) {
    // code within
}
```

Expression is any expression constructed as we discussed earlier. This is called a passive conditional because it allows you to create a statement that doesn't *require* anything on the end of the interpreter. For example, it doesn't require that your interpreter run a code if it comes out that the condition is false. This means that the condition, if necessary, can be skipped over altogether.

However, sometimes you're going to want something else of your statement. For example, if the code runs and it turns out that the statement isn't true, then you can have a backup code that will run in lieu of the conditional code. This ensures that no matter what, an action is always taken, which also gives you an opportunity to create a "backup" clause for your conditional statement by implementing another condition.

The syntax for the active conditional is as follows:

```
if (expression) {
    // code goes here
} else {
    // code
}
```

This will evaluate the expression. If the expression turns out not true, then it will proceed to the else statement, run the code within it, and then proceed to the next part of the program, instead of entirely skipping over the conditional statement as a whole.

However, sometimes you may want to have yet another condition that you can evaluate. This is pretty easy to set up. You can do so through the implementation of *else if* statements. *Else if* statements allow you to easily establish secondary expressions to evaluate. In *else if* statements, the first given expression will be evaluated. If it turns out not true, then the second expression will be evaluated. You can set up as many *else if* statements as you want, but take note that after a certain point, it will stop setting them up over and over.

You can set up an *else if* statement as follows:

```
if (expression) {
    // code goes here
} else if (expression) {
    // code goes here
} else {
    // code goes here
}
```

That is how you set up active conditionals in order to ensure that some codes will always run in a conditional statement. However, take note that this is not always what you wanted to happen. There are many cases, for example, where you may just want to evaluate to see if a single condition has taken place and then retain that code if that's not the case. In these cases, it is better to use a passive conditional.

Arrays

Before we jump into the next part of the control flow, let us first discuss another extremely important concept: arrays. Arrays are a foundational part of programming, and they will inevitably find their way into your JavaScript programming. So, it's important that you understand arrays and how they function for you to be able to write better codes over the long term.

What exactly is an array? An array is a method of storing connected data together in an essential way. The use of an array may not be immediately obvious. Let us first take a look at arrays by imagining a scenario in which they *don't* exist. For example, let's say that we wanted to store all of the different guitar models that we had so that we can easily locate them later.

We could store the names of the guitars like the following:

```
val guitar1Name = "Gibson Les Paul";
val guitar2Name = "Fender Stratocaster";
val guitar3Name = "Ibanez s420WK";
```

As you can see above, this becomes very unwieldy very fast. It can be hard to access the data that you need. Additionally, if you are trying to increment through the data, for one reason or another, like listing all of the guitars that you own, you will have to do so in a sequential manner and slowly work through each variable, printing them out one by one.

This is not the best way to do this. The best way is to do it using an array. Arrays are implemented in many different ways across different programming languages, but the specific implementation of arrays in JavaScript is pretty simple, fortunately. Therefore, you will not encounter many issues in getting them to work, especially as opposed to a language like Java or C++ where they have far more rigid definitions to them which can be more complicated to set up.

Arrays are essentially a set of data, especially in the JavaScript implementation. Arrays allow you to store all of these in a single place and then refer to them by accessing them from that common location. In the original implementation of arrays, you can set up a memory in a contiguous manner such that it will be easy for the computer to refer to these locations and individual value storage locations. All of the data would literally be side by side, which allows you to easily work through this data piece by piece and access what you need instead of messing around with various different variable names and other confusing factors that might further complicate the development.

When you set up an array, you essentially set up individual side-by-side boxes of data, much like the variables that we discussed before. You can then access these boxes by referring to the location of the box. Imagine a bank's safety deposit room. There are several different boxes that you can reach for you to obtain a certain value, and you know which box to reach into by referring to its index.

How can we emulate this in our own code? What can we do there? We can set up our own safety deposit room, as a manner of speaking, and then refer to the box we want to reach into.

In order to do this, you must first declare an array (like any other value) and then feed it a set of data.

var guitars = ["Gibson Les Paul", "Fender Stratocaster", "Ibanez S420WK"];

See how simple that is? Now you can reach into this code and obtain your data any time you want. Let's test this out by creating this file for ourselves. Erase your current JavaScript and type the following:

var books = ["Moby Dick", "Pride and Prejudice", "Ulysses"];

Now, let's say that we want to print the first book from this set. How can we do that? First, we need refer to its safety deposit box. An individual piece of data from an array can be referred to as an *element*. Arrays are composed of many different elements which make up the entire array. These elements are located in different positions in the array, which are referred to as their *indices*, or an individual as an *index*. Array indices start at 0 due to practical computer science reasons that we aren't going to dig into right now.

So, if we want to print the first piece of data in this array, we can do that like the following:

```
var books = ["Moby Dick", "Pride and Prejudice", "Ulysses"];
document.write(books[0]);
```

If you save this and try to refresh your document, you will see the following:

Moby Dick

Easy, right? Know you can locate all the elements in the array. You can also reassign the value of a certain element by referring to its index and assigning it a new value, or you can use this as a means of printing or manipulating the data at these places. Now, let's say that we want to add an element to the array. How do we do it?

The easiest way is to use the *push* method. You simply call the push method and send it the argument of what data you want to add to your array. Let's test this out ourselves. Write the following code:

```
books.push("On the Road");
document.write("<br/>" + books[3]);
```

Save your page and then refresh it. You should see the following:

Moby Dick
On the Road

With that, we've worked through the basics of arrays. You're going to see why this is particularly useful in the next part of this chapter.

Control Flow 102: Loops

What exactly are loops and how can you use them? Loops are an integral part of logic and control flow. You may not realize it, but you use loop logic all the time.

Imagine this: you're sitting there trying to type a text message for your best friend or significant other or somebody. What do you do? It's really simple; you just type each character and then press send, right? But this is an application of loop logic in and of itself.

Think about it. First, you want to type a message, so you open your messaging app. Then, you start typing the message. You seek the character on your keyboard and then you press it and you verify that you pressed the right character. You do this for every character. You also check to see if you typed the final character of the message. Then, you press send and close the messaging app and the loop has been terminated. This is how you can think of many simple activities in terms of loop logic. We tend to not think about this too much because, let's be honest, it's not that fun of a topic to mull over. Regardless of that, it's an extremely important part of loop logic. Therefore, we're going to talk about it nonetheless.

In JavaScript, there are two main kinds of loops, *for loops* and *while loops*. These loops are both similar in terms of their essential logic (do something under these terms), but they have immensely different cases which entails us to use either of them. We're going to spend a bit of time examining these two loops and their optimal use cases in the next section.

Let's start with the easier one – the *while* loop. The while loop is pretty simple because, in a lot of ways, it just mirrors many of the topics that we've already discussed throughout the course of the chapter, specifically the *if* statement. The *while* loop works by repeatedly running through the code contained within it. On every iteration of the while loop, the loop will evaluate the stated condition and determine whether or not it is still true. If it does happen to be true, the loop will run again. The loop will continue to ad nauseum until it determines that the condition for the loop is not true after all. At this point, the loop will terminate and the code will move on to the next point. Hopefully, this is an adequate explanation, but just in case it isn't, don't worry, we're going to be looking at the structure of these now.

So, the structure of a while loop looks like the following:

```
while (expression) {
    // code here
}
```

Let's say, for example, that we want to count from 1 to 10 using this. First, we must define our variable just as the following:

```
var i = 0;
```

Now, we need to set up our while loop. This is going to run for as long as it is less than 10:

```
while (i < 10) {
}
```

On every iteration of this loop, we want to have an *i* increment by one (we'll use a pre-fix so that it prints *i* after it's been incremented rather than a post-fix), and we want to print that increment as well as an HTML line break. The code will end up looking like the following:

```
var i = 0;

while (i < 10) {
    document.write(++i + "<br / >");
}
```

The outcome of this code will look like the following:

```
1
2
3
4
5
6
7
8
9
10
```

However, as you can see above, this isn't exactly the best way to do this. It's a little unwieldy and hard to understand, and you have to go out of your way to do some things that ideally you really wouldn't have to, such as defining a variable that you will use for the loop before you do so.

Loops are useful in checking singular conditions that will become false upon an event. In other words, loops are more preferred if you don't know *how long* a loop is going to run. For a loop like this, where you know exactly how many times it's going to run, it's better to use an incremental loop such as a *for* loop. We'll get to that momentarily.

Based on this, loops are commonly used in the form of a *game loop*. Game loops aren't only for games, of course. Game loops are called so because they follow the basic idea that games do.

A game loop has a certain boolean variable that is evaluated with every run of the loop. For example, you may have a boolean called *running* which is set to be true.

In games, you have a certain win or loss condition that must be met. Until this is met, the same thing will happen repeatedly. For instance, if a player hasn't fallen in lava or been hit three times, then that player is still alive! You don't know how long they'll stay alive, and therefore you don't know how many times you'll need to run your basic logical loop. So, you can't use an incremental loop. It is better to use the *while* loop instead for cases like this.

If you step in lava or your hit counter does hit 3, then you can set the variable running to false. This will indicate to the *while* loop that playtime is over, that the player has lost. Them you can quit running this internal logic and then proceed to the next part of the code, which is a game over screen presumably.

This is a vast simplification but hopefully it does a good job in explaining *what* a game loop is and why *while* loops are so well fit for them. *While* loops are very useful in terms of constantly evaluating a function and repeatedly running the logic in situations where the actual context surrounding it all vary tremendously. If you don't know exactly how much you're going to need to run the code, then *while* loops allow you to check that code for you to be able to obtain a more dynamic interpretation.

While loops are the opposite of *for loops*. *For* loops are used to *iterate* through the code. Instead of just repeatedly running the same chunk until a given condition isn't true, you can define the running terms of the function. This may not immediately make sense, but it will, don't worry.

Earlier, we talked about arrays and mentioned that one of the problems you may run into would be iterating through the guitar variables if you need to. The explanation of the arrays themselves didn't make much sense either in that context. Now, let's dive more into that.

Erase your code for the *while* loop and then bring back the book list code. It should look like the following:

```
books = ["Moby Dick", "Pride and Prejudice", "Ulysses"];
document.write(books[0]);
books.push("On the Road");
document.write("<br/>" + books[3]);
```

Now, let's say that we want to iterate through all these. Remove our write lines so that what remains is our declaration and push method. Then, create a *for* loop. How do for loops work?

For loops work on the basis of iterating through data, as we mentioned earlier. *For* loops have three parts. The first part is the initialization of an iterator variable. This iterator variable serves as the starting point of your loop's "counting". The second part is the condition. This is the condition under which your loop continues to run. This will often be similar to what it would be in a *while* loop of the same function, but sometimes there will be a small change made between them. The third part is the incrementation step. This is the step by which your initialized loop variable moves with every loop of the equation. If, for example, you were to set this to an increment by one (variable++), then on every run of the loop, this variable will change by a degree of one.

The structure of a *for* loop looks like the following:

```
for (initializer variable; condition of running; increment) {
    // code within
}
```

If we want to print every book on our list, what do we do first? Remember that array indices are accessed through referring to their element. These elements start at zero. By starting our initialization variable at 0 and then referring to the index by the initialization variable, we can move through our whole list of books!

Now, how do we define the running length of our loop? In order to define the running length of this loop, you must obtain the length of the array by accessing the array's *length* property.

Then, you must increment by 1 each time.

With all of that in mind, our loop will probably start to look like the following:

```
for (var i = 0; i < books.length; i++) {
    document.write(books[i] + "<br/>");
}
```

Our end code will also look like the following:

```
var books = ["Moby Dick", "Pride and Prejudice", "Ulysses"];
books.push("On the Road");
for (var i=0; i<books.length;i++) {
    document.write(books[i] + "br/>");
}
```

Now, save and run this code and see how it comes out. It should look a little bit like the following:

Moby Dick
Pride and Prejudice
Ulysses
On the Road

With that, perfect! You've made a working for loop in JavaScript. Now, let's talk about functions. Functions are an important catalyst for developing a great working knowledge of JavaScript.

Functions

What exactly *is* a function? A function, to some, may send a person back to memories of their old high school or college math courses where worked with things such as *f(x)* = *y*. In this function, the function *f()* takes an argument of *x*. The argument *x* can be manipulated by the function *f(x)* to produce the output of *y*.

However, there are, in fact, some differences between this definition of a function and the one that we're forced to work with in computer science. Computer science was, in many ways, developed as an extension of mathematics after all. It makes sense that computer science carries over many concepts from mathematics.

How do computer science functions differ? Computer science functions don't just have to take one argument. They also don't have to take *any* arguments. We'll talk about that in just a second. (There are some multivariable functions in higher-level mathematics, but this book isn't going to assume that you have that background.)

Computer science functions can take zero, one, or multiple arguments. These arguments can then be manipulated in the target data to give you a dynamic function to work with.

This is a parallel. For example, let *f(x)* = *3x + 5* = *y*. Let's say that we sent in the argument of *3* for this function. We substitute x for 3 since x is the argument and then obtain our final value y. 3(3) + 5 = 9 + 5 = 14 = y. Therefore, y = 14, and our function *returns* the value of 14.

Just as a function can *return* a value, our own functions can return values too. These functions can be the end result of all of the mathematics and operations that you did in the function. However, a function doesn't necessarily have to *return* anything either.

What is the purpose of functions then? Functions allow you to abstract certain chunks of code in your program that you're repeatedly reusing. This has many uses from a programmer's point of view, but perhaps the biggest deal is the fact that it makes your code more modular. It simplifies and makes things so that you can start using them in multiple different ways even if you use the same chunk of code, without the need for you to repeatedly reuse the code.

Let's work with this idea for a moment. Let's say that we need a function to return the volume of a given rectangular prism. The following is how you define a function in JavaScript:

```javascript
function functionName(arguments) {
    // code
    return value; // (if necessary)
}
```

Let's say that we want to develop a function that can return the volume of a prism. The volume of a prism is just length by width by height as follows:

```javascript
function volumeOfPrism(length, width, height) {
    return length * width * height;
}
```

This will give back the value of the volume. This is one of the coolest parts of JavaScript and scripting in general. Just like any other values in JavaScript, you can save this to a variable and use it later. This gives you a lot of utility and flexibility as a programmer. You can also save it outside of a variable and just print the raw value of the function like the following:

```javascript
document.write(volumeOfPrism(3,4,5));
```

This will print the value 60. You can save it like the following also:

```javascript
volume = volumeOfPrism(3,4,5);
```

This will store the value of volume as 60, which you can then verify by printing it out:

```javascript
document.write(volume);
```

Now, with all of that said, let's cover the last topic. We will not cover it entirely in-depth, but it's important that we do so that you will be aware of what you're dealing with.

Object-Oriented Programming: An Introduction

We're not going to tackle all the complex coding of object-oriented programming right now. We're just going to be dealing with the raw concepts at heart: classes and objects. In order to understand these, we must first discuss classes. This will make some of the things that we said earlier – like object wrappers – make more sense.

What is a class? The utility of classes comes from the fact that sometimes you need more complex structures than what the code automatically gives you. This occurs rarely in languages like JavaScript. Object-oriented programming is about this abstraction at its core: the ability to take smaller concepts and then integrate them into bigger structures that utilize these concepts.

A better way to think about it is to try to imagine a dog. All dogs have features in common; for example, they have 2 eyes, 4 legs, and a wagging tail. They can also bark. However, there can be a lot of variance, too. For example, dogs can have separate breeds and other things which set them apart, like their size or weight.

However, there are still unifying concepts and properties that apply to all dogs, regardless their breed, size, and weight, which are *properties* they all have in common. These can be portrayed as individual data members of a larger structure. This structure can be referred to as a *dog*. These individual data members are called the properties of the dog class. Each class can also have standard functions, like *bark* or *wagTail*, which are common among all instances of the class.

A singular instance of a class is referred to as an object. Each object has its own name and can be treated as its own variable. So, if you define a class *dog*, you can create a dog variable known as *myDog* or

38

any other standard variable name. Then, access the properties and alter them however you wish. This standardization and abstraction are the major appeals of object-oriented programming.

Therefore, whenever something is referred to as an *object*, it means that a class was constructed which consists of smaller data types and pieces of data that all make up the bigger concept that is represented both through the object and through its constituent class.

With that, we've worked through the bulk of the stuff that you need to know as an new JavaScript programmer. These are the foundations of all the knowledge you gained from this book, and it's important that you understand all these before continuing.

Chapter 4

The Future of JavaScript

At this point, you might be wondering, what exactly is the future of JavaScript? What can I expect to gain from learning all these?

Since the whitepaper that brought Ajax to the forefront, JavaScript has only been gaining steam constantly. There are a huge number of new JavaScript frameworks that are being introduced every year that are fantastic for their various different purposes, and more frameworks will be expected.

The future of JavaScript is more about the future of you. JavaScript is only going to become more popular if further features are added into the future ECMA standardizations, if the web in general is used by more people, and if web platforms mature. Likewise, JavaScript matures alongside PHP and CSS. It is expected that JavaScript will continue to develop in the future.

If you want to be a web developer, you must learn JavaScript and be aware of its frameworks, because those will allow you to keep up with the trends.

As technology grows more and more advanced, JavaScript programmers will also be more in demand. There are a number of things right now that are currently relegated to other common scripting languages, like Python, that can be ported to JavaScript. Natural language processing and machine translation are just two examples that will inevitably be ported to JavaScript which therefore increases demand.

JavaScript isn't just for creating pretty web pages; the actual utility of web pages is expanding. With this in mind, JavaScript will advance to this because web pages are now able to perform very complicated actions. The advent of browser-based HTML/CSS/JavaScript games only goes to support this.

As a JavaScript programmer, expect that more programmers will be needed in the industry. Therefore, one of the best things that you can do for yourself is to learn JavaScript and advance your learning.

Conclusion

Thank you for making it through the end of *JavaScript*. Let's hope that it was informative and able to provide you with all of the tools you need to achieve your goals whatever they may be.

The next step is to use this knowledge. Get out there and start working with some JavaScript frameworks. The way to reinforce all that you've learned is by doing it. You won't be familiar with all of them, and sometimes you're even going to be left really confused, but if you keep pushing through, then I guarantee that it will be worth it and you'll come out the other end as a fantastic web developer.

Lastly, if you found this book useful in anyway, a review on Amazon is always appreciated!

www.ingramcontent.com/pod-product-compliance
Lightning Source LLC
Chambersburg PA
CBHW070903070326
40690CB00009B/1970